Dr. Jackson Speaks

Touching A Woman's Heart
(Understanding and Healing Issues of the Heart)

Dr. Cecilia Jackson
"I AM" Fellowship Ministries

authorHOUSE®

AuthorHouse™
1663 Liberty Drive
Bloomington, IN 47403
www.authorhouse.com
Phone: 1 (800) 839-8640

Published by AuthorHouse 09/15/2017

ISBN: 978-1-5462-0625-5 (sc)
ISBN: 978-1-5462-0624-8 (e)

Print information available on the last page.

Any people depicted in stock imagery provided by Thinkstock are models, and such images are being used for illustrative purposes only. Certain stock imagery © Thinkstock.

This book is printed on acid-free paper.

Because of the dynamic nature of the Internet, any web addresses or links contained in this book may have changed since publication and may no longer be valid. The views expressed in this work are solely those of the author and do not necessarily reflect the views of the publisher, and the publisher hereby disclaims any responsibility for them.

All Scriptures used are taken from King James Version of the Bible

Touching A Woman's Heart

(Understanding and Healing Issues of the Heart)

Table of Contents

Introduction
Touching A Woman's Heart
(Understanding and Healing Issues of the Heart)

Cardiovascular disease (CVD) is the primary cause of death in women in the United States (U.S.) and in many other developed and under-developed countries. The words *Issues of the Heart* when used in this text refer to conditions that trouble the heart of women and often cause them to be defeated in life. Parallels are made to CVD because the issues, like CVD, are the primary causes of natural and spiritual death in women.

Cardiovascular disease generally covers four areas: hypertension (commonly known as high blood pressure), coronary artery disease (commonly called blockage in the arteries of the heart), congestive heart failure (a form of heart attack whereas the heart is unable to pump out the blood returning into it fast enough, thus causing congestion in the veins), and stroke (which is a blockage or breaking of a blood vessel located in the brain which results in loss of movement, speech or consciousness). This text will cover two areas or *Issues of the Heart* (CVD): hypertension and coronary artery disease.

Study suggests that an overwhelming number of women in the United States die every year because of specific cardiovascular diseases. The author suggests that likewise, too many women die annually due to emotional and spiritual issues that trouble the heart. The latest trends in cardiovascular disease mortality over the past three decades show that morbidity in women over age 65 has decreased; on the contrary, CVD associated casualties in women ages 35 – 54 have increased. It is suggested that certain risk factors in the daily lives of women may greatly increase morbidity rates of CVD in the near future. Likewise, paralleling this view, the author suggests that the emotional and spiritual death in women is increasing and aggressively invading the lives of women at younger ages. In addition, risk factors in the daily lives of women contribute to high mortality rates and will foster larger spiritual morbidity rates in the future.

It is imperative that Christian women learn to be aware of the risk factors that contribute to these astounding results and begin to diligently learn to cast their cares upon the Lord relieving themselves of emotional and spiritual CVD. There are many examples of women in the Bible who had issues and matters that concerned the heart. God had a remedy for them all and is able to willingly address any issue that concerns you as a woman today.

Although we daily hear astounding data, the power of God is not just hovering over us to break yokes in the areas or issues concerning women; but he is moving superlatively upon, in, and through women of God to bring about change as we push forward in the anointing of the Holy Spirit like a mighty wrecking ball against the walls of issues in our lives that invade our peace with poisons that take our lives. We must replace the poisons with the healing salve of the word of God and the power of purpose that gives vision for destiny and life; then the strength and grace of God will lead God's women as we walk through daily life in victory.

This text *A Woman's Heart (Understanding and Healing Issues of the Heart)* focuses on Biblical answers in response to real issues that concern women of today. The author presents analogies, allegories, and anecdotal episodes that parallel conditions of the natural heart and cures, to conditions of the spiritual and emotional heart of women and cures. Biblical scriptures and solutions are offered.

The author makes no claim of expertise in analyzing the heart as an anatomical organ, instead only general information is presented in this area.

The focus and strength of this work is the presentation of Biblical solutions that parallel spiritual and emotional conditions that concern the heart of women. Avoiding spiritual, emotional, and sometimes physical heart failure has its roots in understanding the Father's love for women since creation. We must first understand who we are which will lead us to victory and understanding and healing our daily *Issues of the Heart.*

Chapter One
A Woman's Heart / Healing Hypertension

Women face herculean issues daily. An *issue* is simply defined as something for discussion or something of intense concern that has the potential to paralyze forward movement in an individual until the problem is resolved or until a solution is found. These herculean issues account for the death of thousands of women in the United States every year. These issues find their lodging places in the hearts of women and thereby can hold them captive, but the Lord always has a path of healing.

Study shows that diseases of the heart, cardiovascular disease (CVD) are the leading cause of death in women and men in the United States. This text uses analogies, allegories, and anecdotal episodes to parallel natural to spiritual conditions in order to establish understanding and strategies for healing the issues of the heart of women.

First, of the four CVD's that we will discuss as a major cause of death in women is hypertension. Hypertension, sometimes called high blood pressure or arterial hypertension, is a chronic medical condition in which the pressure of the blood in the arteries is raised or elevated. This elevation of pressure puts persistent strain on the heart, leading to heart attack and stroke. Even moderate elevation of blood in the arteries is associated with shortened life expectancy. Hypertension is classified as either primary or secondary.

Primary high blood pressure shows no obvious signs of hidden medical cause in individuals with hypertension.

Secondary high blood pressure is caused by other conditions that affect the arteries, kidneys, endocrine system, and the heart. This CVD (as primary hypertension) is rarely accompanied by any symptoms. Sometimes those suffering have indicated the presence of headaches at the back of the head, lightheadedness, fainting episodes, and sometimes visual deterioration.

Let's look at bullet points in summary:

- chronic medical condition
- pressure of the blood in the arteries is raised
- pressure puts persistent strain on the heart, leading to heart attack and stroke
- shortened life expectancy
- shows no obvious signs of hidden medical conditions that affect the arteries, kidneys, endocrine system, and the heart
- the presence of headaches at the back of the head
- light-headedness, fainting episodes, and sometimes visual deterioration
- can be hereditary

An analogy is a comparison of two things that are similar in some respects and have common characteristics. Analogies are often used to help explain something or to make it clearer for better understanding. When making analogies, one often uses similes (the comparison of two different things using the word like or the word as).

This is an example of a spiritual analogy about hypertension. Spiritual hypertension in women is caused by women holding on to issues and not releasing them in personal prayer time in the Lord's presence. It is caused by not trusting in the incomparable love of God. Make no mistakes about it; the results can be identical to the bullet points in the summary above. Hypertension is a chronic, unremitting condition caused by pressure resulting from refusing to cast cares, hurts, anger, pain, and distress upon the Lord and leaving it there. It is caused by allowing circumstances to overwhelm an individual to the extent that trusting God to provide a way of release and deliverance is abandoned. And yes, it can be hereditary. This disease is not selective and will lodge in the heart of any woman who is not cautious. Unless generational iniquities are addressed according to the word of God, this illness will pass on from generation to generation. Some families follow the same anger, resentment, hurts, and pains as their parents in the generation before them. Sometimes these *spiritual diseases* are directed at the same families, friends, or enemies of the previous generation. Carrying accumulated pressure puts persistent strain on the heart, leading to heart attack, stroke, and shortened life expectancy.

Spiritual hypertension, like natural hypertension, is caused by other conditions. Sometimes it's refusing to forgive or holding on to bitterness caused by rehearsing the situation or scene that caused the issue. Often it's refusing to bury the pain and not forgiving one's self. These other contributing conditions can cause an individual to suffer the same symptoms as natural hypertension: the presence of headaches at the back of the head, lightheadedness, fainting episodes, and sometimes visual deterioration.

Analogically speaking, visual deterioration can be the worst of all conditions. When in a state of spiritual hypertension, an individual is unable to clearly see the plan of God for her life, she cannot see past the temporary pain to the permanent peace that comes from letting go of issues. She does not realize the Lord has given victory and peace over them, even while walking through them. Without vision, one perishes.

The recommended cure for medical hypertension is dietary and lifestyle changes. It is noted that compliance in these two areas can improve blood pressure and decrease the risks of other associated health complications. Drugs are prescribed as a cure for individuals with medical hypertension when lifestyle changes are not implemented and effective.

Speaking allegorically, spiritual hypertension is best cured by dietary and lifestyle changes. The diet of reading and applying the word of God and paralleling one's lifestyle accordingly, is the best cure for spiritual hypertension. God's word changes the mind which adjusts the lifestyle

Chapter Two
A Woman's Heart / Healing Coronary Artery Disease

Diseases of the heart, cardiovascular disease (CVD), are the leading causes of death in women in the United States. Coronary Artery Disease (CAD) which is blockage in the heart arteries, also called heart failure or heart attack, is one of the CVD's that greatly impacts women. Heart failure is another kind of CVD. Heart failure is when the heart is unable to provide sufficient pump action in order to maintain blood flow to the heart to meet the needs of the body. This chapter will use an anecdotal explanation to parallel natural to spiritual conditions in order to establish understanding and strategies for healing the issue of coronary artery disease in the heart of a woman.

Coronary Artery Disease is the most common type of heart disease. The disease is caused by plaque building up along the walls of the arteries of the heart. This build up narrows the arteries and reduces the blood flow that goes to the heart. This disease develops when part of the smooth lining inside the artery that supplies blood to the heart muscle becomes hardened, swollen, and stiffened with all kinds of calcium deposits, fat, and inflammatory cells. These build-ups form plaques. Plaques are sometimes described as small pimples or bumps that project forth into the passage of the artery causing the inability of the blood to flow to the heart. A person can have just one, two, or many plaques distributed throughout their arteries.

Early detection of CAD in women is critical for management of the disease and longevity of a quality life. Early detection is sometimes difficult because symptoms are more often noticed in the advanced stages and rarely evident before. A few symptoms are: chest pains due to exertion (angina), a decreased tolerance for exercise, and respiratory distress. Detection using baseline imaging or screening such as: electrocardiography (ECG), stress tests (radioisotope and nuclear) are also methods for early detection. There are others.

It is helpful to know risk factors when considering early detection and prevention. Arteries narrow in the following conditions: aging, smoking, high blood cholesterol, high blood pressure, diabetes, family history, high alcohol consumption, stress (job related or family related), and lack of exercise. If a woman fits the description of one or more of these conditions, you can say these risk factors if not properly addressed can trigger CAD.

Physicians have come up with some common treatments for Cardiovascular Disease and Heart Failure. Below are a few:

- regular exercise
- control body mass weight
- avoid excessive consumption of alcohol
- low sodium diet
- stop smoking
- avoid fat consumption
- statins which reduce cholesterol
- beta-blockers
- nitroglycerin
- stent implantations
- an aspirin regiment

Analogically speaking, one would say the *spiritual* treatment for these problems echoes throughout the word of God. Consider this anecdotal narrative when the issues in life, the issues of your heart, seem overwhelming and spiraling out of control causing spiritual blockage and reducing blood flow to your heart.

A certain woman was greatly crushed and devastated because of the cares of life and the issues in her daily walk that were deeply troubling her and blocking her hope, happiness, and blessings. These issues were causing blockage in the normal flow of blood to her heart. She decided to cast her pains on Jesus, throwing the concern from her heart to him because she knew he loved and cared for her and understood what she was going through. The woman believed he would not allow more to be placed upon her than she could emotionally, and spiritually handle victoriously. She found her escape, her release from despair, by reading God's word and meditating on it day and night. She read his word like a hungry person ate food and found it to be the joy and rejoicing of her heart (Jeremiah 15:16). These actions prevented spiritual CAD.

There were many hard situations this believer encountered, but the Lord was with her through them all. These very situations only made her stronger. No matter what happened, she purposed to be merry, happy, in the midst of the difficulty. This positive, cheerful attitude was like medicine to the woman (Proverbs 17:22, Proverbs 15:17).

Securing her release from the struggle and stress of her issues, she took the time to focus on acknowledging any wrong doing she may have done and confessed her own faults believing God was faithful and would cleanse her from any unrighteousness or wrong doing she may have done. Why? Because the issues we face in life come out of the abundance of the heart and her desire was to have a clean heart no matter what she faced (1 John 1:9, Luke 6:45).

Cardiovascular Disease (CVD) whether hypertension coronary artery disease, congestive heart failure or stroke is responsible for death every minute in U. S. women. Heart attacks by death are more than death by diabetes, cancer, alzheimer's disease, chronic respiratory disease and traffic accidents combined! For the first time in American history death in women due to CVD is higher than that of men. What if more women chose the path of the woman in the anecdotal narrative? We would see changes, help, hope and healing in women throughout our nation and the world.

This is eye-raising information but the power of God is not just suspended over us to break yokes in the area of issues concerning women; but he is moving superlatively upon, in, and through the women of God to bring about change. We must push forward in the anointing of the Holy Spirit like a mighty wind blowing through the daily issues in our lives that impede, weigh down, and even paralyze us from fulfilling our purpose in the Kingdom of God. Furthermore, he has plans for our happiness and personal success in life. We triumph in all things.

Just as physicians have come up with common treatments for physical CAD, God has supplied us with his word that explains myriads of ways to manage and to triumph over the issues of our heart, the concerns about our life, the problems and perplexities we encounter on this journey called life.

The spiritual and most potent treatment for these heart conditions and emotional challenges echoes throughout the word of God. Consider the anecdotal narratives and parallels in this text when the issues in life, the issues of your heart, seem overwhelming and spiraling out of control. These remedies are at least a place of beginning, a starting point, to move forward from spiritual and emotional CVD into better management, understanding, and healing issues of the heart.

Chapter Three
The First Divine Order

In Genesis chapter 1: 26 – 28 and chapter 2, also in 1 Corinthians 11:8, we can read the account of the creation of man and woman. It is important to understand the divine order as God established it in creation before the entrance of sin in the garden. This enables women to know and understand who we are. Knowing the loving God has help for us relieves the heart issues resulting from pressure of others' definition of who we are as women. We become empowered because we know our own worth and identity from the perspective of truth, God's word.

When God first created man and woman, his order was first the creation of man, then the creation of woman.

> Genesis 1:26-27: And God said, Let us make man in our image, after our likeness: and **let them have dominion** over the fish of the sea, and over the fowl of the air, and over the cattle, and over all the earth, and over every creeping thing that creepeth upon the earth. So God created man in his own image, in the **image of God created he him; male and female created he them**.

After creating man, God created woman.

> Genesis 2:7: And the Lord God formed man of the dust of the ground, and breathed into his nostrils the breath of life; and man became a living soul.

> Genesis 2:15-22: And the Lord God took the man, and put him into the Garden of Eden to dress it and to keep it. And the Lord God commanded the man, saying, Of every tree of the garden thou mayest freely eat: But of the tree of the knowledge

of good and evil, thou shalt not eat of it: for in the day that thou eatest thereof thou shalt surely die. And the Lord God said; it is not good that the man should be alone; I will make him a help meet for him. And out of the ground the LORD God formed every beast of the field, and every fowl of the air; and brought them unto Adam to see what he would call them: and whatsoever Adam called every living creature, that was the name thereof. And Adam gave names to all cattle, and to the fowl of the air, and to every beast of the field; but for Adam there was not found an help meet for him. And the LORD God caused a deep sleep to fall upon Adam, and he slept: and he took one of his ribs, and closed up the flesh instead thereof; And the rib, which the LORD God had taken from man, made he a woman, and brought her unto the man.

This was before the fall of man or the entrance of sin into the garden. Therefore, this was the divine order of God for his human creation. The man and the woman were created equal to rule and to reign together over all creation. God blessed them and gave them dominion. Verses 26 and 27 of chapter one, Genesis, reads that God made man and woman to have dominion. He further states that he, God, created both the man and the woman in his image. Both were equal. He even called their name Adam.

> Genesis 5:1-2: This *is* the book of the generations of Adam. In the day that God created man, in the likeness of God made he him; Male and female created he them; and **blessed them**, and **called their name Adam**, in the day when they were created.

The first order of the man and the woman did not suggest superiority of the man and neither did it mean inferiority of the woman. It was simply the divine order in the family as God intended the family to be. Adam was formed first, second the woman was formed from a rib of Adam because God did not think it was pleasant for man to live alone. So he created the woman for the man as his helper (Genesis: 2:18). The word *helper* in Hebrew means adaptable, suitable, and completing. The two were to rule in the garden as partners over God's creation.

> 1 Corinthians 11:8-9: For the man is not of the woman; but the woman of the man. Neither was the man created for the woman; but the woman for the man.

Furthermore, God gave the command to the man to refrain from eating from the tree of the knowledge of good and evil because doing so would cause him to die.

In the first divine order man was created first, second woman was created from the man's rib to be his helper. God called both of them *Adam*. The man and woman were in perfect harmony with God and nature; each was equal and supportive of the other as they ruled their known world.

Women be comforted and encouraged today knowing that God so greatly loved us since the beginning of chronological time that he made us equal in value and worth as a partner with his first human creation and he gave us permission and the authority to have dominion, to rule over everything in our known world.

Remind your heart that you are determined to rule over all situations, and that it does not matter who once loved you and stopped loving you, refused to love you, hurt you because you loved them, or got offended because you would not let yourself be abused by love. Why? Because God showed you a perfect picture of love in the beginning – a picture of what you should desire regarding love – a picture that can ease the issues of your heart concerning love. You are a person of value and worth, and you are capable of having dominion over all that comes against you.

God's idea of true love is in the seed book of Genesis for our purpose and benefit today. It was the first divine order for mankind. Yes, the woman was created from Adam, and second to Adam in the order of creation, but not in the order of position. She was a helper suitable and adaptable, yet she was considered by God as a united equal in priority and authority as the man. He knew the woman could handle the world just as man could. The Bible states both man and woman were created in God's image and blessed and given dominion.

So if we lack confidence and have an issue of the heart about what someone thinks we are capable of or incapable of, we must stand firm in the fact that God thinks we have enough since to rule our known world; so get busy and activate the authority and walk in the victory the almighty God has already given you. He positioned us, along with and beside the man, and ordered both of you to subdue and have dominion over all things. Don't have a heart attack or stress attack about it; subdue and have dominion. Don't take it on as an incomparable problem, subdue and have dominion. It doesn't matter what the issue is; walk in your divine capability and take authority over the issues that agitate and control your very life and health.

We, woman, were in God's mind in the beginning before sin ever entered into the picture of man's life. What is more important, we who have received Jesus into our life are justified from sin, therefore it is as if we are brand new as in the beginning.

The first divine order, a place of perfect love, peace, and authority rests upon you even now. If you are in Christ, you are new. Old things have passed away and all things are new. God will give you the faith and the strength to leave the issues, the pains, and the disappointments of your heart in the place of the old things that have passed. Begin to walk in your God-given divine place of beginning. Water that seed that was planted in Genesis. God has shown women a perfect picture of perfect love and it's still ours today. Who are we? We are women after the first divine order of God because the love, respect and position he had for us was one of equality and value.

Chapter Four
Divine Order After the Fall

Genesis chapter three records the account of the fall of the man and woman from Eden, which means the point in which they disobeyed God which was the first sin. This sin brought about separation of man from paradise and from God in Eden. The scripture says the woman, Eve, herself, confessed that she was deceived by the serpent and violated the commandment of the Lord by eating of the forbidden tree.

God had given the original command to Adam, so the woman was to yield to her husband in this matter of obedience to God's command to him, but she did not.

> Genesis 2:16-17: And the Lord **God commanded the man**, saying, Of every tree of the garden thou mayest freely eat: But of the tree of the knowledge of good and evil, thou shalt not eat of it: for in the day that thou eatest thereof thou shalt surely die.

Because the woman failed to obey the order God gave to her husband and first took of the fruit herself, the order from the beginning of creation was reversed: Eve listened to the serpent, broke the law of equality and plural leadership, and independently ate of the fruit first. Then she fell deeper into error by giving her husband the fruit to eat, and he too ate of the fruit.

The order of creation was altered. The woman usurped authority over the man; the man subordinated himself to Eve because of his love for her therefore both became guilty before God (Romans 5: 12 – 21). The result was judgment on the serpent, judgment on the woman, and judgment on man. The judgment was actually upon the serpent and on all men and all women.

We will concern ourselves with the three judgments on the woman: multiplied conception, sorrow in birth and motherhood, and headship of man over woman instead of co-joint rulership. As we carefully study, we see that even God's punishment on the woman was wrapped in love and the highest form of respect even though she fell in disobedience. Women have many issues, but it is important to pause and study and see the love the Lord has for us that should be the foundation that we stand upon to have the strength to overcome and have hope in spite of the issues we face.

Even God's punishment was wrapped in love and respect. Even though sin and death entered the world by the woman, the forgiving, endless love of God for women persisted and brought redemption by the seed of a woman.

> Genesis 3:15: And I will put enmity between thee and the woman, and between **thy seed and her seed; it shall bruise thy head**, and thou shalt bruise his heel.

God told the serpent there was hostility, resentment, opposition and antagonism between him and his offspring and the woman and her offspring. The seed of the woman to come, would bruise, break, snap, his (satan's) head, and satan would bruise the heel (Hebrew word meaning, the rear of an army). Ancient military history indicates the king's chariot would be at the end of the procession of an army; behind the heavy artillery after the footmen and the archers. At this point in the procession, the way would be clear and safe for the king. Scripture says satan would bruise the heel which is the king that is positioned at the rear of a procession where the way has been cleared for his coming. So satan, through the crucifixion, did the bruising of the king (Jesus). The crucifixion was necessary for man to be redeemed, but it was merely a bruising for out of it, mankind through all ages would be restored to right standing with the Father. Furthermore, the love of God extended to the woman allowed her to be the vehicle through which the savior of mankind would come!

It is clear that the seed of the woman is Christ who came through a woman to break the power, rank, and authority of death, hell, and the grave which was the result of the sin of Eve and Adam. It caused the separation of man from God and blocked the way of salvation for all mankind. But, the woman's seed bruised the head of satan through crucifixion, the descent to hell, and taking the keys to death, hell, and the grave.

The sum of it is, God loved women so much that even though Eve initially caused the fall and reversed the original divine order set by God; the Father's love was strong and resilient enough to use the same woman again and in the most powerful way possible – to birth the redeemer through her seed. Through her body, and her son, the Lord God restored mankind back to right standing with God!

This was her punishment, the pain and suffering of childbirth and motherhood. She, woman, would be the womb that would bring forth the redeemer. What an honorable punishment — to be chosen to bring forth the savior of the whole world! That's how much God loves women. Even his punishment was love! What manner of love is this? It is incomparable. Eve had a huge fault, a huge issue, but the love of her God was greater than her failure and granted her forgiveness and that with honor.

Women, what does this mean to us regarding our issues and the things that concern our heart? We must stop belly aching over the failures of our past. Dismiss the dress rehearsals that cause the old scenes and characters of your life to be played over and over again. The mistakes, errors, failures, hurts, disappointments, and our perceived obvious insufficiencies belong in the sea of forgetfulness. God has already seen, understood, forgiven, and moved past our past. He knows the pain and the disappointment we have in ourselves and our personal fall, but he has already marked us as those who will provide the way, whose testimonies will bless others. He has already declared our womb, a birthing place for life and for being a conduit for the healing of other women.

Satan only bruised our heel, but that which will come through us resulting from our process through life and its trials will bruise, break, snap, satan's head. Go forward in the power and authority God has freely given to you.

God chose to use us, women, to redeem both the man and the woman and to restore man back to the image of God, from the place where he had fallen.

> Isaiah 7:14: Therefore the Lord himself shall give you a sign; Behold, a virgin shall conceive, and bear a son, and shall call his name Immanuel.

> Isaiah 9:6-7: For unto us a child is born, unto us a son is given: and the government shall be upon his shoulder: and his name shall be called Wonderful, Counsellor, The mighty God, The everlasting Father, The Prince of Peace. Of the increase of his government and peace there shall be no end, upon the throne of David, and upon his kingdom, to order it, and to establish it with judgment and with justice from henceforth even for ever. The zeal of the Lord of hosts will perform this.

> Galatians 4:4-5: But when the fulness of the time was come, God sent forth his Son, made of a woman, made under the law, To redeem them that were under the law, that we might receive the adoption of sons.

God used a woman to bring forth his only begotten Son, the savior of the world. He did not use the seed of a man although the savior would be a man, but the seed of woman to initiate the New Creation Order whereas, a woman brought forth the Man, Christ to enable all men to be a new creation acknowledging the passing away of old things and ushering in the new! **The new redemptive order in the family is: Christ, the man, the woman, the children, hence – the order**

of the Christian family! Men and women are redemptively equal, but functionally different. In redemption, Christ is the covering and loving care and protection of his wife.

> Ephesians 5:23-31: For the husband is the head of the wife, even as Christ is the head of the church: and he is the saviour of the body. Therefore as the church is subject unto Christ, so let the wives be to their own husbands in every thing. Husbands, love your wives, even as Christ also loved the church, and gave himself for it; That he might sanctify and cleanse it with the washing of water by the word, That he might present it to himself a glorious church, not having spot, or wrinkle, or any such thing; but that it should be holy and without blemish. So ought men to love their wives as their own bodies. He that loveth his wife loveth himself. For no man ever yet hated his own flesh; but nourisheth and cherisheth it, even as the Lord the church: For we are members of his body, of his flesh, and of his bones. For this cause shall a man leave his father and mother, and shall be joined unto his wife, and they two shall be one flesh.

Because of the woman, redemptive order was brought to the church through Christ. The new redemptive order of the church is: 1) Christ (the redeemer, headship, covering, loving care, and protection of the church); 2) The Church (the woman who is submitted to, loves, and gives herself to Christ). The Church figuratively represents both men and women who are believers. The Church is also figuratively, the woman. She is to honor her husband and submit to him and he to love her as Christ loves the Church.

What an awesome punishment; a punishment of love and respect that changes old patterns and establishes a new order! How much love, how great is His love for you? Greater than any other; he forgives, gives a second chance, leads and guides. Remember, he knows the pain and the disappointment we've had in ourselves and our personal "fall", but he has already marked us (like Eve) as one who will provide the way that will redeem others. He has already declared your womb, a birthing place for life and for other women. Satan only bruised our heel, but that which will come through us will bruise, break, and snap his (satan's) head giving us total victory.

Chapter Five
Go Forward

The Lord has given us the power, authority and rank to break through and go forward! It does not matter what chains seem to hold us, we have the power to go forward in freedom.

The word of the Lord to the women of God today is the same word given to Moses and the children of Israel when they faced the Red Sea. When we face issues, red seas in our lives, places that are hard and when there appears to be no way of breaking the wall; God says go forward in the face of the situation. Begin to walk forth and God will open the sea for you.

In other words, God will change the situation; he will bring resolve and deliverance in areas adversely impacting your heart. The difficulty, obscurity, and impenetrability will be reversed and become simplicity, opportunity, and clarity. God is a heart healer, only go forward! The Lord will fight for us when we have no energy left. Sometimes the fight is holding your peace while he makes a way, but you will find your feet on dry ground, deliverance, right in the midst of the issue! And when the Lord brings deliverance, the deep issues in our heart (the Egyptians) that we face today, we will not see them again anymore, forever!

> Exodus 14:13-16: And Moses said unto the people, Fear ye not, stand still, and see the salvation of the Lord, which he will shew to you to day: for **the Egyptians whom ye have seen to day, ye shall see them again no more for ever. The Lord shall fight for you, and ye shall hold your peace.** And the LORD said unto Moses, Wherefore criest thou unto me? speak unto the children of Israel, that they **go forward**: But lift thou up thy rod, and stretch out thine hand over the sea, and divide it:

and the children of Israel shall go on dry ground through the midst of the sea.

This is the recording of the actual narrative of victory.

Exodus 14:19-30: And the angel of God, which went before the camp of Israel, removed and went behind them; and the pillar of the cloud went from before their face, and stood behind them: And it came between the camp of the Egyptians and the camp of Israel; and it was a cloud and darkness to them, but it gave light by night to these: so that the one came not near the other all the night. And Moses stretched out his hand over the sea; and the LORD caused the sea to go back by a strong east wind all that night, and made the sea dry land, and the waters were divided. And the children of Israel went into the midst of the sea upon the dry ground: and the waters were a wall unto them on their right hand, and on their left. And the Egyptians pursued, and went in after them to the midst of the sea, even all Pharaoh's horses, his chariots, and his horsemen. And the Lord took off their chariot wheels, that they drove them heavily: for the LORD fighteth for them against the Egyptians. And the LORD said unto Moses, Stretch out thine hand over the sea, that the waters may come again upon the Egyptians, upon their chariots, and upon their horsemen. And the LORD overthrew the Egyptians in the midst of the sea. And the waters returned, and covered the chariots, and the horsemen, and all the host of Pharaoh that came into the sea after them; there remained not so much as one of them. But the children of Israel walked upon dry land in the midst of the sea; and the waters were a wall unto them on their right hand, and on their left. Thus the LORD saved Israel that day out of the hand of the Egyptians; and Israel saw the Egyptians dead upon the sea shore.

Concluding, the Lord says to women, the issues in our heart that need healing and have lingered in our lives for so long will be trampled under our feet and we will no longer see them dominate in our lives forever. God, the Lord Jesus, the King gave us a decree to go forward!

Chapter Six
Women in the Bible / Healing Heart Issues

As stated in the introduction of this book, the focus and strength of this book is the presentation of Biblical solutions paralleling spiritual and emotional conditions. Avoiding spiritual, emotional, and sometimes physical *heart* failure has its roots in understanding the Father's love for women since creation. It is first understanding who we are that leads us to victory, and understanding healing of daily issues of the heart. It is realizing that we can search the scriptures, our pattern for life, and hear the voice of the Lord concerning matters of the heart as women.

Let us take a glimpse through the pages of God's word to see how God is impartial and comes to the support of women concerning the matters that concern them. He gets involved when something is wrong or not working properly, and when something is upsetting or causing alarm of any particular kind. He cares when something persists in our lives and is contrasting with what our heart desires. The Lord, Himself, becomes the defendant in these matters and steps in to make a difference. He does not always do this as a matter of normal procedure or expected action; often it is apparent that the action is divine intervention. Divine determination and intervention in the face of our uncertain circumstances is the supernatural power of God superseding the natural and thereby, causing a divine result.

The day-to-day life of women has been recorded during the centuries in Biblical accounts from the early days after creation to the latter days of the first century. A challenge understanding the daily lives of the women we read about in the scripture is remembering that these were real people with real hopes, concerns, issues, problems challenges, and skills and gifts.

Women in Bible times were not just two-dimensional characters based on fictional literature. Their lives moved at a slower pace in terms of technology, but they faced inconveniences that are unimaginable in our modern Western culture of today. It took them days to do some of the things we push a button and accomplish today. Therefore, their strength in the midst of life required brawn and brains simply to survive daily challenges.

Their lives are inspirational examples to us because of paralleling points of identification: finding husbands, raising children, living happily with their husband and family, cooking, shopping, cleaning, surviving in social systems (the poor and the wealthy and those in between), learning to live in cities, learning to live in rural areas, dealing with crime and delinquency in communities, dealing with travel, business of buying and trading goods, menstrual cycles, mood swings, coping with their changing technology from wood to clay to metals, moving through the seasons of life (from young girls to teens to women), and raising families of their own while dealing with health matters (although they had a shorter life expectancy than we), and being caught between generations trying to care for extended family even as they are trying to build their own. They experienced so much more than time will permit this text to cover. Certainly, there are paralleling points of identification. So, how did God divinely intervene in the lives of these women in order to speak to us today? These women in Biblical times were no different than us; they had real issues.

Previous chapters in this text have taught about Eve, the first woman. Prominent female figures such as Ruth, Hannah, Mary, and Esther are often the topics for texts about women. This text will glimpse into the lives of only a few prominent women but primarily focus on some powerful, but less prominent women in the Word.

Chapter Seven
Brief Encounters / Women in the Word and Issues

We can search the scriptures, our pattern and Book for life, and see examples of how women trusted the Lord concerning matters of the heart. Most of what women of the Bible experienced was similar to what modern-day women experience. God is impartial regardless of the era in time, and comes to the support of WOMEN concerning the matters that concern them. The Lord gets involved when something is wrong or not working properly, upsetting, or causing alarm of any particular kind. He cares when any matter disrupts our lives and is conflicting with what our true heart desires. The Lord, Himself, becomes our advocate in these matters and steps in to make a difference.

As we are studying the daily lives of a few women from the Bible in this chapter, remember these were real people with real hopes, concerns, issues, problems, challenges, skills and gifts just as we are real women today. What God did for them, he can and will do for us because these women were not just two-dimensional characters based on fictional literature; they were real live examples from the past that give us hope for today. They are prototypes. The examples in this chapter are brief and present great insight and light on female Biblical figures. Some are less prominent; yet, the powerful messages in their stories are equally as strong as prominent figures.

Sarah
Issues of the Heart
Sarah, the wife of Abraham, was old in age and past the season in life for childbearing, yet she wanted to bear a child for her husband. She laughed to herself thinking at first it was impossible for God to perform a miracle for her because it was biologically impossible.

God had promised them a child twenty-five years prior and the promise had not been fulfilled. Yet, the time had come for the fulfillment of the promise. Even Abraham, her husband, had lost hope of receiving a son from Sarah and was satisfied with Ishmael another child by a concubine. He begged of God to accept Ishmael as the promised child. God said explicitly that the son of the promise would be the son of Sarah. Sarah became impatient, faithless, desperate, and frustrated which led her to great sin. When faced with this kind of heart matter, she did what some of us would have done. She sought a solution within herself because she had adapted herself to the customs of the Egyptians, the culture of the people immediately surrounding her. She suggested Abraham take Hagar, the Egyptian maid as a concubine. Trouble arose in the home: Hagar developed a spirit of superiority; Sarah (not accepting the fact that she was the source of the problem, did not repent) blamed Abraham. Truly, Sarah had an issue of the heart.

The Miracle – the resolution

Divine intervention and the forgiveness of God prevailed. Sarah's time of waiting came to an end. The Lord visited not only Abraham, but also Sarah and established the promise. The next year after the holy visitation to Abraham, Sarah gave birth to Isaac just as the Lord had said. Even in the midst of the horrible issue, God's spoken word prevailed and Isaac was born. The scriptures record that by faith even Sarah received the ability to conceive though past the proper time of life. In other words, she was too old to have a baby. (See Genesis 21: 1 – 13, and Hebrews 11:11.)

Remember, Sarah was an ordinary woman with ordinary emotions and the stigma of being barren which led her to desperate issues, but God was faithful and he will likewise be faithful concerning us. The issues today are not beyond the reach of our loving Father. Our barrenness in some areas of our life may cause us to be impatient, desperate, faithless, despondent and frustrated. We may even be weakened to the level of beginning to think like the world around us, but we must not give up on God. Like Sarah, in spite of the times we have acted foolishly and given birth to an Ishmael, God delivered to us the promise and will continue to do so.

Miriam

Issues of the Heart

Miriam was an intelligent child. Her mother entrusted her with an assignment of caring for her younger brother, Moses. She did so by connecting her mother, a Hebrew woman, and an Egyptian princess; resulting in her brother Moses being rescued from death. This benefited both God's people and the Egyptian house of the time.

Miriam was a woman of stature as an adult, a woman of courage and faith. The family of Amram and Jochebed was unique in Israel's history because it brought forth three great leaders who served the nation at one time: Moses, Aaron, and Miriam. Miriam (along with Aaron) assisted Moses in leading God's people out of Egypt to Canaan. She was nearly the age 100 when the miracle of the Red Sea occurred and she became a leader of women in dance and worship to God for his triumphant victory.

Miriam was an unmarried woman called by God to exceptional tasks: she was the first female prophet, spokeswoman for God; her life was totally centered on loving God and his people; her gifts were not for just the smaller families in the tents of Israel, she was called to an entire nation. Miriam was a born leader, a strong woman. Leadership came easily to her. Without a doubt scriptures support women as mighty leaders for God. The problem is Miriam's very strengths became issues and weaknesses.

The root of the biggest heart issue was with Moses. Moses, the great leader of the Israelites, was Miriam's younger brother and his second marriage was to an Ethiopian woman. What is in one's heart will eventually be spoken audibly, and the heart issue in Miriam eventually surfaced.

Matthew 12:34: O generation of vipers, how can ye, being evil, speak good things? For out of the abundance of the heart the mouth speaketh.

Luke 6:45: A good man out of the good treasure of his heart bringeth forth that which is good; and an evil man out of the evil treasure of his heart bringeth forth that which is evil: for of the abundance of the heart his mouth speaketh.

Miriam found Moses' marriage to an Ethiopian, difficult to accept. Perhaps she felt Moses was out of order to be a man of God and to marry a woman from another nation. Perhaps Miriam was reacting to the fact that another woman was entering the life of her younger brother, thus creating hidden jealousy (especially since she was unmarried). Was she upset that he was happy with a foreign woman when she felt countless other Israelite women would have been more suitable for his wife? Was she concerned about how the marriage would affect the people of their nation and later cause trouble for him as leaders? Was she upset because at that time in history relatives, including adult siblings, usually decided upon matters of marriage and her younger brother by-passed the normal process? These questions are not answered and maybe one could say they are proper spiritual reactions from a mature woman; but spiritual reactions from someone mature would have first considered what God's intents were for the nation rather than just the emotions and issues of a blood sister - brother relationship. Miriam had issues that troubled her heart.

Miriam's issue had at its core, the fact that she had ascended to the highest position ever held by a woman in Israel and she was named a leader by God in the same breath as the two male leaders. Having a sense of equal opponent status, she simply overstepped her boundaries. She simply overestimated her authority. She considered herself to be on the same level as Moses and therefore challenged the choice of God's appointed man for the appointed time. In her posture of pride, she undermined his authority and even asked him if it were not true that she and Aaron were his equals.

Aaron could not resist his sister's dominating authoritative manner so the two of them tried to usurp Moses' authority and by doing so endangered the unity and future of the entire nation of Israel and God's message for us, spiritual Israel. This action could have impacted generations. To reject Moses was to reject God because God had chosen and appointed Moses, and God was using Moses to make a generational statement about interracial relationships. To reject Moses' choice was to interfere with God and Moses. It was not meant to be a triangular decision (God, Moses and Miriam), but a decision instituted by God through Moses as his proxy.

Although Miriam was a chosen and exceptional vessel of the Lord, herself, somewhere things had begun to shift in her attitude with regard to her position and authority. She shifted from God's control to self-control. No doubt these changes occurred subtly and she did not realize that her heart and motives were changing, nor did she consider the consequences of such shifting.

God's response was Miriam fell sick with the dreaded disease of leprosy. This illness would cause her limbs to decay and eventually fall off. She could no longer live among her people and would eventually die. Leprosy is paralleled to spiritual decadence, sin.

Seeing his sister a leper, and hearing the once joyful voice of melodious praise turned to the shrill cry of "unclean", caused Aaron to immediately repent from the "foolish" act and sin. Then he begged Moses to save Miriam from death. Moses then cried to the Lord asking to heal Miriam of the deadly disease. He asked God for his sister's deliverance, and healing; he asked for her life to be spared. He asked God to forgive her foolish sin. Moses forgave Miriam for her sin against God and him, and became her advocate before God.

The Miracle – the resolution

Moses did not rebuke his brother and sister, but he prayed asking God to heal Miriam from leprosy (her sin). Aaron, the high priest, was out of spiritual position to pray because he was indirectly part of the problem and responsible for her fall; but Moses pleaded with God for Miriam's healing. He interceded for her. The prayer of Moses changed a lifelong sentence of suffering to a sentence of only seven days!

That's how much God loved his daughter Miriam, even in the midst of the foolishness of her heart issues that caused her disfiguring fall. God forgave her and healed her and sentenced her to only seven days outside the camp of Israel. Seven is Biblically, the number of perfection and completeness, and is used over 600 times in the Bible. God made a perfect, complete and final decision concerning his compassion for Miriam. He used her to establish a disdain for racial superiority, even when it comes to Israel. He used a woman to establish a principle doctrine establishing his approval of racial diversity.

The miracle – the resolve is God restored her! God revoked, canceled his own lifelong sentence of pain that leads to an ugly death and replaced it with a seven-day chastisement then released Miriam to come back to the camp of her people in health! (See Exodus 15: 19 – 21 and Numbers 12: 1 – 15.)

It would be wise for a woman to not fall into the sin of pride, the sin of thinking more highly of herself than she should, racial superiority or the sin of rebelling against a leader appointed by the Lord; however the awesome thing about our awesome God is that he loves deeply and he forgives deeply. The issues of the heart were not too deep for the reach of God's love.

The issues of Miriam's heart led her to a place of pride, sin, and poor health; but God's love for her led to answered prayer and healing streams reconnecting her to a place of safety, security, family, and hope. Surely the matters of your heart's concern and not beyond the healing reach of our loving God. One of God's most powerful, chosen, female leaders had fallen, but the almighty God of all creation came to her rescue as he will always come to our rescue.

Bathsheba
Issues of the Heart
The story of Bathsheba and David reveals truths about another woman in the Bible whom God finds a way to bless and honor, in spite of what she has to encounter on her journey. Her heart issues were very painful but not beyond the comfort and healing of the Spirit of God.

Traditionally, Bathsheba has been blamed for her adulterous relationship with the king of Israel, but when one reads 2 Samuel 11 – 12, contrary to popular understanding, the Bible is clear that this woman was innocent and a powerless recipient of King David's lust.

The setting of the narrative is in the spring when kings would go off to war, but David sent Joab out with the Israelite army and the king's men; but he remained in Jerusalem. Actually, David had no business in Jerusalem while his men were off to war. This was not the natural nor spiritual culture of Israel at the time, thus he was not in alignment with God's will, but vulnerable to the leading of satan. Having taken time off from war, he was walking on his roof and saw a woman bathing on her rooftop.

Only when you study and understand history and culture can you conclude that Bathsheba was not intentionally orchestrating a plan to lure the king. Her common knowledge would lead her to believe, David would not even be on sight, nor would most of the able bodied men. They would have been gone out to war. So, David actually spied on Bathsheba and went further with his lust and sin by asking one of his men who was left to attend to him, to bring Bathsheba to him. In other words, he involved another person in his ugly lust and sin.

David was not deterred from this lust even when he discovered Bathsheba was a married woman. He slept with her, and then sent her back home. In contemporary words, he used his power and position and sent for Bathsheba, raped her, then sent her back home with the pain and burden of it all. Later, the woman discovered she was pregnant and sent word to David.

Keep in mind a woman's position in those ancient times. This era was hundreds of years before the birth of Christ. Women could not testify in court, they could not appear unescorted in public venues, they could not talk to strangers, unmarried women were not allowed to leave the home of their father, and women had little or no authority. It was only God's intervention that brought women of that time into places of position and acceptance where women were able to be seen as individuals and leaders who played necessary roles in their own right.

This gives greater appreciation for Jehovah and his determination in the Old and New Testament to set patterns for women today to be free from the bondages of gender restraints. Many restraints held Bathsheba in a most difficult situation and forced her pain to remain deeply hidden only in her heart. She had a deep and hurting issue of the heart, especially since she was pregnant with the result of her perpetrator.

Know that Bathsheba had no rights to refuse the king. No doubt, she was in fear for her own life and was not happy that she became impregnated with his child because this would reveal what would be a grim picture for the kind of woman others would think she was. The Bible says Bathsheba loved her own husband.

This woman, Bathsheba, was merely an object of desire, a channel for David's own lust, and prey for his yearning and sexual appetite. Therefore, Bathsheba became an innocent victim then, just as women now who are rape victims in today's society often become innocent victims with few options other than to suffer in silence unless someone cares enough to reach out and minister to their hurt and pain.

Sometimes these women are victims of fathers, uncles, their mother's boyfriends, male relatives in the family and in the church, even brothers and sisters in the family.

God help our societies and communities because sometimes these innocent victims are viewed as the guilty ones, the ones who stimulated and motivated the sick characters who victimized them. Like Bathsheba who was victimized by the king, they are afraid and don't know who to tell. If this is the source of some of your issues today, the Lord has come to heal the matters of your heart. Praise to the Lord our Healer.

As the story continues, when Bathsheba sent word toDavid he responded by having Joab (one of his men) bring her husband back from war so he could sleep with his wife, hoping the man would believe his wife was pregnant by him. This way David could cover up the fact that he used Uriah's wife unjustly, and against the natural and spiritual laws of Israel. Bathsheba's husband, Uriah, was an honorable Hittite. He refused to come home and sleep with his wife while his commander and general and the rest of the men were still on the battlefield. When David could not cover his sin and guilt, he fell into deeper sin by having Bathsheba's husband killed in battle.

Bathsheba loved her husband. The Bible says she mourned for him when she heard he was dead. This left this woman in a very difficult position. She had no covering and was pregnant.

David, after murdering her husband, sent for Bathsheba to become his wife and she had no real choice other than to be passed from one man to the next like an animal – a cow or goat. But the Lord was not pleased and intervened.

Some women today have been like cows and goats to men: passed from one man to another for what ever reasons, but the Lord is not pleased and will intervene for them if they desire for him to. Whether an innocent victim of rape or a victim used by choice while looking for love in all the wrong places; the Lord loves you. If this sounds like some of your issues, come out of hiding and know that the Lord loves you and will intervene on your behalf and heal your broken heart and heal the emotions and issues surrounding the pain you carry. He whom the Son sets free is free for certain. You do not have to carry these hurting, painful issues of the heart.

The Miracle – the resolution

God sent the prophet, Nathan to David and rebuked him through a story that revealed all he had done. The prophet told an allegorical narrative of how Uriah had a wife and children and shared everything with her and she slept in his arms and he loved her. He told how a rich man refused to take his own sheep, but took the little lamb (his wife) that belonged to the poor man, and prepared the lamb for himself. The story Nathan told shared how Uriah treated his wife with love and respect, yet David treated her as cattle to be traded or sold.

Nathan prophesied (2 Samuel 12: 8 – 9) of how God had given David all of Israel and Judah and would have given him more if that were not enough. The prophet then rebuked David for killing Uriah.

The Bible records that David repented (Psalms 32; 51) and God forgave him and his relationship with God was restored, although no one could change what had already happened to Bathsheba and Uriah. God was still faithful. David became a gentle, kind and loving husband to Bathsheba trying to make the best repairs for the sins he had committed. God gave Bathsheba Solomon, who became a great man of God and was known for his wisdom and for building a temple for the Lord. Bathsheba loved her son in spite of the shameful way he was conceived. And God healed her heart as only he could. Solomon eventually inherited David's throne.

Women of God, there are things in all of our lives that we wish we could re-construct, re-do, re-live; but there is a season to weep no more over the past and to go forward to the existing, bright future of the promises of God. There is a season to let go of the issues that trouble our hearts and let them have no more dominion over our lives. We must yield to the power that Christ is releasing in us to overcome and yield to the "new thing" he is doing in our lives, healing our issues of the heart.

I am sure it is true that Bathsheba had painful moments in her dysfunctional past from the rape to the death of Uriah, to the thought of being pregnant and having to move into the house of David, the man who had taken advantage of her. Yet, as she continued to live, forgive and trust God, peace came and the blessings of giving birth to Solomon brought her joy in spite of her past sorrows.

Remember, this was an ordinary woman with ordinary emotions and extraordinary pain which led her to deep issues, but God was faithful and he will likewise be faithful concerning you. The issues and matters of your heart are within the reach of our loving Savior and he will heal the broken hearted and take you through the issues of your life to the waters of healing and victory.

The Woman at the Well
Issues of the Heart

During Christ's lifetime, women (and men) were engaged in unhealthy relationships. Women used their influence over men for evil purposes because they were dependent on men for their safety and livelihood. Men also abused their power over women. The story of the woman at the well is a popular narrative about the matters of a woman's heart.

The story began with Jesus and his disciples travelling from Judea to Galilee. On the way, they passed through Samaria and stopped outside the village of Sychar.

Normally, Jews avoided contact with their Samaritan neighbors by going a longer route around this country because they were ethnic enemies and had a long history of violence, prejudice and discrimination. Such conditions exist in today's society, which makes this narrative quite current. Jesus' team of followers went through Samaria intentionally as it seemed Jesus was looking for a special woman with whom to dialogue.

While his disciples had gone to the heart of the town to buy food, Jesus stayed behind as the omniscient Christ who knew the certain woman he was looking for would be coming to the well to get water. Breaking all cultural norms, he had conversation with the woman. Note that according to Jewish tradition, men did not speak to women in public, even their own wives. Also, a teacher (rabbi) which is what Jesus was, would not even think of talking to or teaching a woman of poor reputation. Yet, here Jesus sat at the well anticipating her coming and determined to talk to her.

Jesus, as in all cases within the Gospel accounts, did not treat women according to Jewish cultural laws and adaptations. Instead, he set patterns of teaching women, talking to women and addressing women's issues. He trusted women to proclaim his word, and the message of the Kingdom. Unfortunately, these are patterns neglected by some in Christian organizations today.

The woman at the well was an ordinary woman who had neither money nor influence. We know this because she was carrying her own water vessel to draw from the well. She had a hard life and had been unfavorably involved with at least six different men (John 4:18). However, Jesus pulled this woman into relationship by asking her first for a drink of water. This positioned him as the one who was in need. The Master was strategic because he shifted the conversation from the topic of physical water to spiritual water and he revealed the secrets of her heart about her being used by men looking for love in the wrong places. Today, we would equate her to a prostitute or community whore, or adulteress.

The Miracle – the resolution

As Jesus and this unusual candidate for conversation discussed details about where to worship, Jesus revealed to the woman that there would come a time when men would worship God in spirit and in truth. Apparently the Samaritan woman heard about Christ's coming and told Jesus that she knew that Messiah, called the Christ, was coming and he would explain everything to them about life worship (John 4: 17 – 21, 23 – 26). This was a firm and bold confession of her faith in the coming Messiah. Because of her great faith, Jesus responded to her telling her he was the one she was speaking of. In other words, he said he was the Messiah she had so much faith in; therefore proclaiming that he, Messiah, was speaking to her there at the well.

This woman knew she was speaking to the one who would cause her to never thirst again. She knew she was in conversation with the Messiah! So, she left the well and carried the news back to her village. This made her one of the first woman missionaries to carry the Gospel to those who had not heard it. She carried the Good News to Samaria! Yes, Jesus chose to use a woman who had serious issues to deliver the precious Gospel to mankind! In a few moments of time, of honest discourse, Jesus changed a woman's perspectives, forgave her of her past, re-started a new present and future for her, and then plunged her into ministry! That's powerful and so radical. This deliverance was representing the love of the Lord towards women, even women with issues. He resolved them quickly.

Women of God, stop focusing on your issues and focus on how God wants to use you for in His Kingdom! If a modern, traditional church were choosing the appropriate, ideal candidate to be a missionary to evangelize a new group of people who need to know Jesus, it is not likely that they would choose a person with issues like the woman at the well.

But Jesus looked past her culture, his culture, and her issues and saw this woman as the ideal person to carry the Gospel!

The key is she was honest with him in confessing that she had no husband, so he could trust her and bring out further truth that would heal her and deliver her from her issues and lead her into believing and receiving the Christ, the Son of the Living God. Then he sent her forth into ministry.

Consider the fact that the issues in your life and your past life, do not go unnoticed by the Father. Jesus intentionally went to Samaria to have an encounter with this woman just as he intentionally seeks after you to have an encounter with you and your issues. The matters of your heart are not too bad, too sad, too weighty for the Lord to solve them as he reveals himself to you. Then in the spirit of forgiveness and love he will heal you and thrust you forward into the Kingdom work of spreading the good news and being used for the ministry he has created you for. He heals issues of heart, specializing in *Touching A Woman's Heart.*

The Crippled-Bowed Woman

To be crippled or bowed means to be physically disabled to the extent that one is unable to walk. Anyone who is *crippled* is said to have an illness or infirmity, frailness, or medical condition that is debilitating. This crippled state can be to the extent that one is bowed or bent over without the ability to stand straight.

Do you have a concern that causes you to be **spiritually crippled,** unable to continue to go forward, so paralyzed that you can't seem to go on with your life and the freedom and peace that comes with being a child of God? Do you have a weakness that causes you to bend with shame or pain to the extent that you feel your issue, your hurt is obvious to others, but you can't do a thing about it. Maybe you don't feel it's obvious to others, but you cower over in fear and pain when you are alone and have lost your backbone to stand up and face particular challenges in your life? If this is your issue, the Lord heals and forgives the crippled. Being spiritually crippled will cause you to waste years of your life when you could be standing and living a happy, victorious life.

The Miracle – the resolution

There was a Jewish woman, a daughter of Abraham, who had been crippled since the age of eighteen. She was unable to straighten her back and was bent over. Once Jesus was teaching in the synagogue and he called her forward and healed her from this illness, telling her she was loosed from the sickness. The Greek language paralleling *infirmity* means a malady or a weakness in the body or mind. It is also considered a disease or frailty. The Bible states when Jesus called the woman to him, and laid His hand on her and told her she was loosed from the condition, the woman then stood straight up and began praising God (See Luke 13: 10 – 16). Usually when there is a physical malady, there is simultaneously a mental malady that is the source or the partner working together keeping an individual bowed, crippled, and broken.

It does not matter the issue that seems to be crippling you, Jesus is the healer who will enable you to stand straight up and walk through it and bring you healing even to the point that your heart and spirit will rejoice and glorify God! Your physical body and your mind can and will stand up when the Lord Jesus heals you. He is the only one who can dig deep into the core of a woman and labor with her to heal issues of the heart.

Woman Caught In Adultery

Adultery means disloyalty, falseness, betrayal, deceitfulness, faithlessness, unfaithfulness, and infidelity. It is voluntary sexual relations between a married person and somebody other than his or her spouse. I challenge you to see this issue the way God looks at it.

There are times when our issues, concerns, and the matters of our heart stem from **spiritual adultery**. We may not have affairs with anyone other than our spouse, but we can betray, become disloyal and deceitful to the Lord Jesus Christ. We engage in intercourse with other things that we make gods in our lives (family, children, careers, ministry, entertainment, fashion flair, spouses, gifts, hobbies and more). The Bible declares that Christ is the bridegroom and we (the ecclesia, the church) are his bride.

We are spiritually married to Christ, yet there are times when we show disloyalty and betrayal by spending more time with others than we do with him, making other people and things priority rather than putting him first. We are often deceitful because circumstances can sometimes overwhelm us and we forget that he knows all things and we cannot hide any behavior nor any thought or attitude from him.

There are times when faithlessness and unfaithfulness creep into the days of our lives and we find ourselves not trusting in him and not believing he is able to fulfill every promise to us. This is spiritual adultery and God has given an example in his word of how much he cares for us even when we fall short in this area.

The Miracle – the resolution

The adulterous woman was brought to Jesus by the scribes and Pharisees having been caught in the act of adultery. They claimed that the woman should be stoned, according to the Law of Moses. These religious people hoped to trick Jesus into saying or doing something that would bring a charge against him; but, Jesus simply responded by saying that whoever had not sinned should throw the first stone at the woman. One by one the woman's accusers left, leaving the woman alone with Jesus. Jesus then told her to change her ways and mend her character. He forgave her of adultery. (See John 8: 3 – 12)

Jesus forgives us of adultery – even *spiritual* adultery. He just needs some of our time alone with him. If adultery is the root issue of your concern, go into your secret place and spend time alone in his presence. Just as Jesus proved to the religious people that others have sinned, we must understand that others fall short in areas of their lives also.

Get quiet with God, repent. He forgives and charges us to change our ways and mend our character, then to move forward.

Jesus asked the adulterous woman where her accusers were. Her response was there were none. Jesus said neither did he accuse her and he asked her to go and not to sin again. If adultery is the root issue of your concern, whether literal adultery or spiritual adultery, you can change and Jesus says go and sin no more. If it is the underlying matter of the condition of your heart, Jesus has the cure for adultery. Simply repent and prioritize his patterns in your life. Prioritize time with him and it will help to reshape your character. Go, and sin no more.

Abigail

A matter of the heart that concerns some women is similar to that of Abigail's: she was **married to a man who was spiteful and lacked wisdom**. In fact, the Bible calls him a fool. This woman had to survive in a household with a man of this personality in a culture where she was not equal to men and the weight of her welfare depended upon the foolish man. But Abigail was wise and beautiful and the Lord guided her with strategy to live victoriously with her husband in the midst of a set of issues that could have destroyed her. He will do the same for you if this is one of your issues. Abigail had to assume the leadership and headship role in her home during a very dangerous and unique situation. This woman of God proved to be wise, discerning, influential, timely, judicious and extraordinarily effective. Her wise response to his foolishness changed her condition and that of her household from a mess to a miracle.

Abigail was a beautiful, wise wife of a wealthy man named Nabal. David and his soldiers protected Nabal's flock and shepherds from thieves. Once, David's leaders requested supplies from Nabal in exchange for their military help. Instead of giving the supplies, Nabal insulted David's men in every way possible according to ancient rules of hospitality. This caused David to be offended and very angry, so he and his 400 men prepared to fight against Nabal.

Nabal's servants told Abigail of the impending catastrophe. She did not consult her husband, but ordered servants to load up bread, wine, seeds, and cakes of fruit onto donkeys and she led a supply caravan to David's camp hoping to assuage him and his men and to stop a war. Abigail even apologized to some of David's fierce soldiers for Nabal's reckless, imprudent behavior and offered the gifts. She also reminded David of his anointing from God and suggested he not shed unnecessary blood which could cause God to be offended with him over Nabal's disrespect and ignorance.

The Miracle – the resolution

It could be said that Abigail's beauty, diplomacy, and the gift of the food she brought, won the victory. David took her advice and did not pursue revenge against Nabal.

When she returned home, Abigail said nothing to her husband because he was drunk; but the next morning she told him the truth. Approximately ten days later Nabal suffered an illness like a stroke and died. David did not delay marrying Abigail. God blessed her with a warrior and a king as a reward for her Godly wisdom.

It's amazing that God has examples in his word for matters concerning women. God gave Abigail strategy for her situation, and he will do the same for you. Notice her beauty was an asset and not a curse. Be proud of how God made you, even if others may resent it. Believe that God will assist you during hardship even in a situation when the man as your mate is spiritually immature and incapable of effectively serving in his place of headship and authority in your home. The Lord is still ever present to help you and anoint you to function in any necessary role that will give you victory as his daughter. He specializes in *Touching A Woman's Heart*.

Notice God gave Abigail specific strategy for how to win the heart of the army and how to find favor with David. Expect God to give you specific strategy in your dealing with an unwise man or mate. He has plans and will grace you with diplomacy specifically for your need. He will make your business his business if you let him. Notice in Abigail's case, God removed the heart of the problem, Nabal. I am not suggesting that God will allow terminal illness to come upon a person to resolve your issue. What I am suggesting is that God loves you enough to intervene for you and go to extreme measures to help you and answer your prayers. Absolutely no issue that concerns your heart is beyond God's power to reach and change.

Deborah and Jael

Deborah was a strong and courageous woman who lived during the era when judges, rather than kings, ruled Israel. Deborah was the only woman with the official title of judge in the Old and New Testament. Her story is amazing. She was not only a female judge but she was a leader of Israel's army. The culture of Deborah's day did not support her serving as a leader in the nation, but God supported her and used her as an example for women today. God supported courageous, strong, wise, female leaders then and supports us now! Step out of your fears and insecurities and go forward in Kingdom purpose.

With God's help, Deborah was successful against all odds. Her story is one of God's delight in using those who are weak and insignificant to accomplish his will on earth, so it will not be said that man gives victory, but only God gets the glory for victory in our lives (1 Corinthians 1:27 – 28).

1 Corinthians 1:27-31: But God hath chosen the foolish things of the world to confound the wise; and God hath chosen the weak things of the world to confound the things which are mighty; And base things of the world, and things which are despised, hath God chosen, yea, and things which are not, to bring to nought things that are: That no flesh should glory in his presence. But of him are ye in Christ Jesus, who of God is made unto us wisdom, and righteousness, and sanctification,

and redemption: That, according as it is written, He that glorieth, let him glory in the Lord.

In the same way today, God will come to our aid and sustain and reinforce us in a culture and in some church political systems where being a woman leader is not always popular nor accepted. God has chosen to use women, the *weaker* to confound, bewilder, baffle, and amaze (in the Hebrew: to disgrace or dishonor) those who think they are mighty and wise. We women are candidates to be used just as Judge Deborah, the leader of old, was used to bring victory to her people.

As a judge and prophetess, for decades Deborah held court under a palm tree in northern Israel. The children of Israel came to her for solutions and judgment because her gender would not allow her to judge in proximity with the other male judges.

Today's women (as was with Deborah) do not need a traditional pulpit to proclaim the word of God, although God by his omnipotent power is opening the male dominated pulpits. We, like Jesus and his apostles, use the market place, communities, and anyplace where our feet walk as our pulpits and the power of the Lord goes before and with us. Therefore, women of God do not hold on to issues and the pains in your heart as a result of offense, abuse, neglect or suffering resulting from a male dominated world or male dominated church world. Since God is for you it does not matter who is against you.

> Judges 4:4-5: And Deborah, a prophetess, the wife of Lapidoth, she judged Israel at that time. And she dwelt under the palm tree of Deborah between Ramah and Bethel in mount Ephraim: and the children of Israel came up to her for judgment.

Deborah judged and executed exceptional militaristic leadership (Judges 4 – 5). She was victorious in battle as a leader of Israel. During the centuries after God delivered Israel from Egypt, the people of God went through seven renunciations of their religious belief and allegiance to

God. Israel fell far away from God and suffered many wars and great oppression. Judge Deborah is one of the deliverers God raised up to save Israel and she was a woman.

The Canaanite, King Jabin, and his commander Sisera tyrannized and demoralized Israel for twenty years and finally the people cried out to God for help. So, God told Deborah the strategy to defeat the Canaanites. Deborah gave the orders to her commander, Barak who was nervous about the odds against Israel because they were vastly outnumbered. Despite Deborah's command and military position, Barak doubted her judgment as a woman. He refused to fight unless she went with him (Judges 4:8). Deborah agreed to go with him, but flowed into her prophetic mantle and told him that because of his manner of disrespect and his non-compliant approach, the honor of the victory would not be his as the commander, but God would give the honor to a woman (Judges 4:9).

The Miracle – the resolution

As Deborah prophesied, the Canaanites were defeated. All were killed except Sisera, King Jabin's commander. Sisera ran and hid in the tent of Jael a Kenite woman, thinking he would be safe there because the Kenites were at peace with the Canaanites at the time. However, Jael was not a friend of the Canaanites and Deborah's prophecy was fulfilled. While Sisera was sleeping, Jael hammered a tent peg into Sisera's skull, killing him.

In Judges Chapter 5 verses 24 - 27, Deborah sang a song of thanks to the Lord for delivering the Israelites from the Canaanites. It is the oldest poem found in the Bible. Throughout the poem, Deborah recounted miracles God had done for Israel. In several stanzas she gave praise to Jael for her bravery in saving women of Israel from rape, robbery, and vandalism which would have been the result of a Canaanite victory. Because of the courage of two women, Israel lived forty years in peace and prosperity.

Like today, the culture of Deborah's day did little to support her serving as a leader of her nation, yet she served effectively with God's help. So will you as a woman of today who has been called to lead. Deborah led her nation's troops victoriously against a vastly outnumbered group of soldiers. Likewise, you will lead triumphantly against all the forces of the enemy that have been dispatched against you, your family, and your kingdom assignment.

Furthermore, remember Jael was an unmarried woman all alone in her tent who brought down a powerful commander of the enemy's army; a single woman. What are the matters that concern your heart as an unmarried woman? We have an example of the power of God solving them. Like Jael, we can be all alone in a tent, yet we are not all alone because the Lord is with you and even when no one is around. We have the courage of Jael to drive a deadly stake through the head of our enemy rendering him useless! You will triumph victoriously over him! You have a God who causes you to triumph over every issue that tries to plague you.

The Lord says to drive a stake through the head of every enemy that comes against you. When you decapitate the head, the source and all that comes with it is rendered useless. For example: when you decapitate fear; then intimidation, anger, sadness, uncertainty, cowardice, lack of confidence, and other attached spirits will be useless and of non-effect in your life. Go forth with the courage and might of Jael. Every tactic and trap sent by satan must bow to the authority and dominion of Christ in you. Drive a stake in the head of your known enemies. You are not alone, for the Spirit of the Lord, the Warrior is with you.

Remember God chooses the simple things of the world to bring shame to those who think they are wise and strong and he chooses the common and humble things to bring down the haughty. There is no issue in your life, no matter of concern, that the Lord cannot reach with his heart of love and his hand of miracles. You are a woman chosen to triumph in every matter of your heart.

Junia

In Romans, Chapter 16, the Apostle Paul takes time to introduce many of the called leaders and brothers and sisters of the faith. There are over fifteen names mentioned. Among them is Junia. Junia is Biblically named an apostle.

Some Bible translations write the name as *Junius*, a male spelling. Other Biblical and historical evidence indicates Junia, Paul's relative, as female. Scripture also indicates Andronicus and Junia (the female spelling) were among the apostles and were believers of Christ even before Paul, himself, was a believer. They also experienced imprisonment because of their faith.

Some scholars also suggest that Junia was the wife of Andronicus. Paintings and drawings of antiquity also portray Junia as female.

Junia was named among the apostles of the New Testament. Although a woman, she was an apostle. The Lord did not leave us without an example today. He set truth into the pages of his word that clarity would be evident and without controversy today. God called women to be leaders, judges, prophetesses, and also apostles.

> Romans 16:7: Salute Andronicus and Junia, my kinsmen, and my fellow prisoners, who are of note among the apostles, who also were in Christ before me.

Jochebed

Are the issues of your heart similar to those of Jochebed? She was a **woman who had to give up her own baby** to save its life. She knew it was not best for her to keep him because of the conditions and circumstances of the Hebrews at the time. I am sure it hurt her heart to have to let him go, but it was a decision that she knew was a better situation for her baby.

Jochebed was a Levite, the mother of Miriam, Aaron, and Moses. She was married to Amram (not unusual at that time, he was her nephew).

Jochebed gave birth to her children during an era when the Israelites worked hard as slaves for the Pharoah of Egypt. Despite the treacherous, perilous, unstable circumstances of the time, the family still loved and followed Jehovah, God. When Pharoah decreed all Hebrew male newborns to be killed, the family of Jochebed and Amram refused and hid their youngest child, baby Moses for three months (Hebrews. 11:23).

They were not afraid of the king's commandment; but when they could no longer hide Moses, Jochebed coated a basket with tar and pitch (terrain from the ground) and blended it to close the holes in the basket, making it an ark for the baby to lie in. She hid her baby along the banks of the Nile River in the make-shift ark (place of safety designed by God).

Jochebed's daughter Miriam stood guard over the child because Jochebed could not bear to watch and her heart was hurting seeing her own child leave her arms and the comfort of her family to be placed in the dangerous Nile in order to save his life from death by the Egyptian Pharaoh.

The Miracle – the resolution

Only the heart of a mother could understand the joy and relief Jochebed felt when Pharoah's daughter came to the river to bathe and saw the baby in the ark and requested her maid bring the child to her. When the daughter heard the baby crying, she actually sent her maid to find a Hebrew woman to nurse Moses. The woman brought back to nurse the child was actually Jochebed, herself. Pharoah's daughter paid her to nurse her own baby. Only the heart of a mother can understand the joy Jochebed must have felt being able to nurse her baby without Pharoah killing it; on the contrary, only a mother could understand the pain she must have carried knowing that when the child grew older, she would have to go and give her child back to Pharoah's daughter who claimed Moses as her own son (Exodus 2: 1 – 11; 6:20; Numbers 26:59).

Moses later saved his people, was one of Israel's greatest prophets and leaders, led the children of Israel from Egypt and the Israelites through the wilderness, received the ten commandments, expedited the instructions for the Tabernacle of Moses) and also wrote the Pentateuch (first five books of the Bible). Jochebed could not see Moses' future, but she trusted God and because of her audacious, courageous faith in God's ability to preserve her child, a nation was rescued.

The Bible does not state whether she ever had close relationship with her son, Moses, or conversed much with him again; but, we note her as a woman who had a real issue, a real matter of the heart and God met her need. She could not have saved her child against the decree of Pharoah, if she didn't want a better life for her son, so Jochebed decided to move in faith and give her child up to the divine providence of God. God met her need; he saved Moses' life and in doing so, rescued a nation as well.

Some women reading this literature can identify with Jochebed. Some know of other women in their circle of relationships who can identify with Jochebed in several ways. Just remember the end result was good and even great because the Glory of God and advancement of the Kingdom of God, resulted from the foundation of Jochebed's decision.

Some women have actually given their child or children up for adoption because they knew the outcome in its situation would be terrible. Maybe death by a symbolic Pharoah, a certain socio-economic poverty, a physical or mental or family dysfunction, or perhaps their own lack of maturity and mind set at the time concerning rearing their baby. God says let the pain go from your heart and embrace the peace and rest in Jesus, knowing the plan of God for that child is good and even great. Let go of the guilt.

Some women are trusting God that he will be the ark in the dangerous Nile River where their children have put themselves, in spite of their parental warnings not to go into that river. God says trust the fact that their end will be good and even great. Sometimes, just like with Moses, God will even use Pharoah to bring your beloved child (adopted or spiritual children as well) to greatness. It may be through pain and in some cases the suffering of loss, but the final result will be good.

For some women, it is an idea or ministry or business or some fashion of a dream they have carried and given birth to and the Pharoah had decreed that it will not live. Call the Pharoah assigned to your dream a defeated foe. Build an ark for your business, your ministry, you plan, and let it float on the waters. God will make of it a good and even great thing and if he must, he will use Pharoah's daughter (someone who is not even a believer and has no love for the true and living God) to help bring to pass the destiny and purpose God has for your child, your Moses. Hallelujah!

There is no matter of the heart that God cannot and will not heal for us. Look ahead and know that your Moses will live, and an even greater purpose will unfold. Jochebed prayed and trusted Jehovah even beyond the fear in her heart. Pray and trust the Lord. He can and will direct our seed even while they are in an ark on the Nile. He will divinely manipulate the situation and life will come to the thing(s) we've birthed. From the pages of Biblical history, the Lord has always reached in and touched a woman's heart.

Chapter Eight
Conclusion

Study suggests that many thousands of U.S. women die every year because of specific cardiovascular diseases, hypertension and stress. The author suggests that too many of these women die annually due to emotional and spiritual issues that trouble the heart.

Furthermore, the author believes the emotional and spiritual death in women is increasing and stress related risk factors in the daily lives of women contribute to these high mortality rates. These stress related issues are pains in the heart of a woman that only the Lord can touch. It is imperative that Christian women learn to cast their cares upon the Lord relieving emotional and spiritual CVD. There are many examples of women in the Bible who had CVD, issues and matters that concerned the heart, but God had a remedy for them all.

The power of God is not just hovering over us to break yokes in the area of issues concerning women; but he is moving superlatively upon, in, and through the women of God to bring about change as we push forward in the anointing of the Holy Spirit like a mighty wrecking ball against the walls of issues in our lives that invade our peace with poisons that take life. We will replace the poisons with the healing salve of the word of God and the power of purpose that gives vision for destiny and life; then the strength and grace of God will lead God's women as we walk through daily life in victory. We are the voices that speak into the lives of other women who do not know Christ, that the love of Jesus will also heal their hurting and broken hearts.

This text, *Touching A Woman's Heart (Understanding and Healing Issues of the_Heart)*, is dedicated to using Biblical narratives as answers and responses to real issues that concern women today. The focus and strength of this work is the presentation of Biblical solutions to spiritual and emotional conditions of the heart. Overcoming spiritual, emotional, and sometimes physical heart failure has its roots in understanding the Father's love and healing for women since creation. It is about understanding who we are that leads us to victory. As we, God's women of his word, embrace his truth and learn to walk in overcoming victory, then we become conduits to carry change to the women of our communities, our nation, and the world, proclaiming the power of the Lord that Touches a Woman's Heart.

Bibliography

Bevere, John P. Victory in the Wilderness. Apopka: Messenger Press, 1991

Daniels, Kimberly. Spiritual Housekeeping. Lake Mary: Charisma House Publishing House, 2011

Elefteriades, John A., Caulin-Glaser, Teressa. The Women's Heart Book: An Owners Guide. USA: Prometheus Books, 2008

Freeman, James M. Manners and Customs of the Bible. Plainfield: Logos International Press, 1972

George, Jim. 10 Minutes to Knowing the Men & Women of the Bible. Eugene: Harvest House Publishers, 1977

Howard, Beverly. Treasures of the Heart. Wooster: Cincinnati: Lexis Publishing LTD, 2013

Jackson, Michael, Jackson, Cecilia. Who is God?. Cincinnati: "I AM" Publications, 1986

Karssen, Gien. Her Name is Woman. Colorado Springs: The Navigators New Press, 1987

Meyer, F. B. Abraham (The Obedience of Faith). Ontario: Fleming H. Revell Company, 1983

Mindell, Earl L, Hopkins, Virginia. Prescription Alternatives. Stamford: McGraw-Hill Publishers, 2003

Books Published By The Authors
Drs. Michael & Cecilia Jackson

1. 9 Gifts of the Holy Spirit
2. A Synopsis: Differentiating Religion, Tradition, Church, & Kingdom
3. A Woman's Heart
4. Be Made Whole
5. Belonging
6. Beyond The Veil
7. Bold Truth
8. Breaking The Curse of Poverty
9. Get Her Back on Her Feet
10. Categorizing Spiritual Gifts
11. Dialogue Between the Watchmen and The King
12. Discern Deploy The "Heir" Force
13. Dominion For Practical Singles
14. Don't Feed The Bears
15. Finding The RIGHT Woman
16. From Press To Passion
17. Go-Forward!
18. God's Woman of Excellence For Today: The Shunammite Woman of II Kings
19. Hannah
20. It's A Wrap!
21. Kingdom Quest I
22. Make Your Valley Full of Ditches
23. Rebuilding the Economy of the Global Kingdom of God
24. Releasing The Leader Within
25. Simply Praise
26. Step Back To Sprint Forward
27. The Bible Mesmerizing, "In-Your-Face" Info
28. TRU - The Tongue of the Learned for Cultivating Racial Unity
29. Tithing Your Tithes
30. Tool Kit for Understanding Prophets and Prophetics in the Church

31. Wailing Women Warriors Win
32. Who Is God?
33. Who Is The Holy Spirit?
34. Write To Publish (Scribes)!
35. You Have A Gift

Printed in the United States
By Bookmasters